Soulmates

Mark Anthony

Books by Mark Anthony

The Beautiful Truth

The Beautiful Life

Love Notes

True Love

Love Lines

For my one and only Bird,
my soulmate, light, and love of my life.

Part 1.

You won't believe in soulmates,
until you meet yours.

Be patient.

Know the pain isn't forever.

Birds still sing.

The sun still shines.

The mountains still stand tall.

And no matter how long it takes to heal, there is still a love inside you that is forever, and always.

When you find the right one,
your heart will be calm,
and your loneliness will be gone.

You will trust they are the one
sent to you by the universe
for your soul to grow, and
because the love is real,
there will be times
when it will be hard
and it will hurt
because life has pain,
but you will still know
they are the one for you,
and there is no better place
for your soul to be.

I will hold you
until everything
broken inside you
falls back
into place,
until everything
mixed up,
abandoned,
and lost,
finds
its way
back home.

She's tired of being taken advantage of.

She's tired of holding on to nothing,

She's tired of not being a priority.

She's tired of lies, promises and games.

So be the one she can rest her head on.

Be the one that lets her sleep.

You're finally at
peace with
yourself,
comfortable
and beautiful
in your own skin,
so find
somebody
who can see it,
appreciate it,
and add to it,
not somebody
who is going to
take it away.

It doesn't matter if
she's reading a book,
sleeping,
or planting flowers in the rain,
I always see the grace in her
movement,
the infinite in her smile,
and the tenderness in her heart.

Soulmates stay together,
not out of fear of being
alone,
but out of the joy
of being together.

I hope the love
you're searching for finds you,
exactly when you're ready,
and not a moment too soon.

The ocean taught her to believe
in the wonder of mystery,
and the patience of sand.

It taught her to listen to her heart,
and to feel the salt water on her skin.

The ocean taught her to believe
in the miracle of life,
and the simplicity of letting go.

The ocean taught her
that happiness
comes and goes like waves,
but life always stays beautiful
to a heart that knows the ocean.

She is like the universe,
a great mystery
that can't be solved by science,
and her beauty is like the moon:

Just look at how she illuminates
everything, no matter how near,
no matter how far.

Without her,
the sky is only
spilled ink.

A poem,
yet to be written on
earth.

There is no end to the way she
amazes me,
how her slightest touch
makes me feel like a child again,
naked and vulnerable to the world,
but this is what it means to be alive,
and in love,
and constantly reborn,
into the sunlight of her kisses,
and the moonlight of her smile.

If you made a mistake in
looking for love,
forgive yourself,
for what is more human
than wanting to find love?

What is more beautiful,
even if it didn't work out?

Nobody has ever succeeded
at anything,
including love,
without failing first.

So forgive yourself,
and move on to where
you are meant to be,
and love will find you.

She began to see
life like a poem,
and when a child
handed her a flower,
she saw it
as more than just kindness.

It was innocence itself
handing her all the beauty
in the universe,
and asking nothing in return.

She wanted more.
She felt trapped.
She felt hurt.

But she kept fighting
for herself,
until she became
courageous and strong,
and capable of moving on.

She became the hero
of her story,
and the muse
of her own magic.

Physical attraction
is only part of the formula:
you need laughter,
music, food,
and friendship.

You need honesty,
trust, humility, and a
willingness to walk
together
through the fire.

One day
all the
heartbreak
in your life
will be
nothing more
than a distant
memory,
and the love
of your life,
will be
the love
of your life.

On a sunny day,
there is nothing to do,
but let the breeze do its work.

Let the sunlight spread
across your face in golden kisses.

Let the peace of summer sink
into memory,
so that when the rainy days come,
and the cold water drenches you
where you stand,
you will remember
that sunny days always come
back,
as bright and beautiful as this.

Relationships that
last are at times
as difficult as
those that
don't;

It is a question of
whether or not
this is the one
with whom
you want to
do the work.

People want to be perfect
in the eyes of others,
but we're all works in
progress.

So better to go forth,
wearing your imperfections
on your sleeve,
and apologize for nothing.

Because one day
you will find somebody
who loves you, exactly
as you are, and you
will look back and
realize,
everything has always
been perfect
in its imperfection,
including you.

Don't worry about the past
or you will destroy the present,
making a new past you will regret.

Learn to live in the moment,
without the worry that keeps you
from enjoying the taste of a strawberry
or the whistle of a singing bird.

Can you really see how gracefully the
light is coming through the windows?

This is a unique moment in time,
even with all its mad uncertainty
and hope,
and you can never get it back.

Just look at how the light is always
reaching out to touch you,
no matter how many times you turn
away.

She taught me to be confident in
what I know,
and humble in what I don't;

She taught me to laugh at my mistakes,
and be proud of my triumphs.

She taught me not to let praise
fool me into believing my work
is done.

She said to keep creating
no matter who likes it,
and not to see the world
through the eyes of others.

She taught me to be as bold as a child
who isn't afraid to pick his favorite color,
and hold it closely to his chest.

She's done chasing better versions of
herself, acting as if she isn't perfect
as she is.

She's tired of taking herself back to the
store as if she's broken, flawed or not
what she wanted.

From now on, she's going to take
herself out in whatever condition
she's in,
and rise like a kite
above the rooftops.

From now on,
she's going to say,
"I love being this crazy damn kite,
and there is never going to be another
one like it again."

You won't have to chase
your soulmate,
because true love finds you
when you are ready to
receive its gifts.

I wish I could write
a poem that made me
feel,
the way you make me
feel
behind closed doors,
when not even the moon
can speak.

I still live in gratitude
of everything she's
given me,
and I'm still humbled
by her kiss.

Nobody escapes childhood
without some scars to
remind them of where
they've been,
and where they need to heal.

But if you know this,
you can learn to be patient
with yourself and others,
as everyone is fighting
some hidden battle,
and trying to recover
the beauty of innocent things.

Even in love,
there are bad days
when things don't go as planned,
but you learn not
to judge a bad day
as a bad relationship.

You see how moods
can come and go like the weather,
and just being aware of this,
will help you stay together,
and in love.

Travel isn't a destination, but
a state of mind.

Sometimes,
when we're drinking coffee
or walking hand-in-hand
in our home town,
we'll have the same smiles
on our faces,
as we had in Paris,
and we feel the same
romance
running like a river
between us,
and even though
Paris is a million miles away,
love is still everywhere we look.

Never stop being the real you.

You are brave and beautiful.

Be kind to yourself.

Take each day as it comes,
and don't worry so much
about the future.

Things have a mysterious
way of working out,
in the end.

It's never too late to begin again,
and create the life and love,
you've always wanted.

Driving home the other
night with the radio on,
and the moonlight
chasing me in the
rearview mirror,
I thought of you,
and all the times
you've made me laugh,
smile
and shake my head.

And every love song
I sang along with that night,
no matter how beautiful,
silly,
or sad,
was a song about us.

Before we met,
we both wasted time
with loves that didn't last
and hearts that didn't open,
because true love is something
that has to be experienced
to be believed,
and nobody knows
what it really
means,
until it walks
through your front door
and says,
"I always knew
it would be you."

I love walking with you by the ocean,
as the sunlight kisses the water,
listening to the voices of our children
playing in the sand.

The ocean reminds me
of how time passes,
and how so many things can change,
yet some beautiful things,
no matter the wind or tide,
always remain the same.

You won't forgive yourself
for your mistakes,
until you start to see them
as the lessons you needed
to grow into somebody
strong enough to love
and be loved,
through all seasons.

She will never be at peace with
the world because she cares too
much about those who suffer,
and feels too much of other's pain,
but she will find a way to be at
peace with herself,
and not add to the pain of others.

She will find a way to become
like sunlight,
coming through a field of wheat.

There was a time
I was afraid
I would never find
my soulmate,
but once I decided
I wouldn't settle
for anything less,
I had no choice
but to trust one
day it would
happen,
and then one day,
when I wasn't
even looking,
it did.

To have a broken heart
is to know you're
capable of love.

And if you're capable
of loving once,
I promise you,
you're capable of loving
again,
only more deeply,
and wisely than before.

Don't waste your time trying to love
somebody who isn't right for you.

It only prolongs the pain
of not being with the one who is.

It's the simple things that
mean the world.

Sunlight, rain,
flowers, and coffee.

Your smile in
the morning.

Your laughter in
the evening.

Your kiss before sleep.

I am thankful for all the gifts you
bring into my life.

You, the holder of my heart.

You, the compliment to my soul.

You, the one I dream of,
even when I am awake.

You, the one I wished for,
even before I knew your name.

She deserved the world,
but didn't see the beauty
of her own beauty,
until one day,
she found the mirror
inside of herself
that showed her the truth
that is always true,
and the beauty
that stays beautiful
to everyone with eyes to see.

Wait for somebody
who loves and
appreciates
all the different parts of you,
from the silly to romantic,
from the shy to the insane,
the artist, the outlaw,
the inspired one,
the lazy one,
the lover,
the one who is waiting
for somebody
exactly like you.

She has a voice like rain
falling against a blue window,
and after love making,
she whispers in my ear
all the secrets of poetry.

She knows the importance of moonlight
and tea, mismatched stockings,
and clouds.

And sometimes our bed will rise into
the night sky,
and take its place among the stars,
where she says I can always find her,
if I just believe.

Before we met,
I didn't believe in magic
or miracles,
but now that forever
is spreads out like blanket
between us,
and the sky is blessing us
with blue,
I can say I believe in magic,
and miracles,
and it is all because of you.

Take your time being single,
and figure yourself out.

Find out what you love,
and what inspires you.

Find out what makes you smile,
and laugh,
and what fills your heart
with joy,
so that when your soulmate
arrives upon your doorstep,
they will know it's really you.

Don't lose sleep over
anybody who isn't
dreaming of you.

Don't lose sleep over anybody
who doesn't know your secret
heart.

Go back to sleep,
and dream a new dream,
and know that when
the right one is
dreaming,
they are dreaming
of you.

So many words of advice,
and so many books
on how to help somebody
in a bad relationship,
when the only thing that helps
is being so tired of being tired,
you are ready to do
whatever it takes to move on,
and the funny thing is,
by then
you won't need anybody's advice,
but your own.

She steps into a new day,
knowing that whatever happens,
if she slows down for a moment
to experience it,
it will be beautiful.

Just a breath,
and a moment to take in,
a cloud,
a river,
a rainy street.

Everything is a poem
waiting to be written
into the soul,
by anyone with eyes
childish enough to see.

This dance we do,
this tango, this salsa,
this raw electricity of life
pulsing through our bodies
like lightning.

Some beats break our hearts,
and some melodies make us remember
how just one moment
of dancing on this earth together,
can be so
beautiful,
even the stars
will watch in envy,
as we glide,
dip,
and fall in love.

You are the secret oxygen of my planet,
the sunlight of my shadow,
the flower that always makes my heart smile.

Yesterday is a done,
a picture you can look at
but never bring back,
so find the flower of today,
and smell it deeply
before it becomes another
scentless thing
that can only remind you
how beautiful it was
only yesterday.

You will find peace
with the right one,
so deep,
you will be able to
sleep through a storm.

PART 2

She wanted somebody
who would look at the stars with her,
and not have to say a word to know
what they meant.

Somebody who knew
why some beautiful things
are doubly beautiful
when silently shared
with somebody you love.

Bring me your day-to-day,
your boredom
mixed with roses,
your speedy kisses,
and burnt toast in the morning,
and I will love every color,
every wrinkle,
every minute,
every passing glance you give me,
as it turns cold coffee
into love.

We found each other like
two shipwrecked souls on
an island of dreams.

Your face woke me
to the sunlight, the trees,
and the birds,
and I was no longer thirsty
for anyone but you.

And sometimes still,
in the quiet of dawn,
I will touch you gently on the shoulder,
to make sure I am still dreaming,
and that this dream is real.

When I told you
that you were the love
of my life,
I knew I would
have to spend
the rest of my life with you
just to prove it.

Between the earth and the stars,
I find the delicate spaces
where our love lives like the breath
of the universe,
waiting to exhale,
and in that moment,
my heart is filled with every treasure
a man could ever want,
and I know for certain
why a poet will always be
wealthier than a king.

I never long to be
with other women
because she
is every woman to me,
a mad lover,
and a quiet teacher
with a tender heart.

She can change
from rain to snow
to sunlight,
all in a single day,
and so I am faithful to her
because I know
she is as infinite
and lovely,
as the universe,
and there is no end
to her mystery.

Some days
you
pass
through me
like wind
or mist
or some mystery
I can't solve,
and I am left
only
with a yearning
to be near you,
to feel the heat
that gives me
life,
and blesses
my days
like sunlight
upon the ocean.

When you meet
the right one,
it will change
everything
you thought
you knew
about love.

All lasting relationships,
including soulmates,
require work,
and feeling
and sometimes
it's hard to feel
because it hurts,
and so we numb
ourselves with phones
and cigarettes,
and football games,
hoping to play it safe,
but feelings
don't go away until
you feel them,
and so you must keep
feeling, and talking,
and living,
in order to stay in love.

You must earn your soulmate,
again and again and again.

After so much time together,
we've created our own private language
full of tired jokes and obscure
references, rare phrases
that can only be deciphered by us.

Ours is a language born of
shared experience, laughter,
and time;
it is a language of whispers,
memories,
and secret codes of the heart.

This is our language of the soul,
and it will never be spoken again
by anyone else on earth.

You don't have to wait to love yourself.

You don't need permission to do things
that make your heart open,
and your soul sing.

Sometimes you will have to be
your own soulmate,
so that another soulmate can appear.

She's fire,
and lace,
mystery,
and sunlight.

She's a question,
and an answer,
and an endless sea.

She's everything
the universe
wants to dance with,
and when she dances,
she dances with me.

If you haven't found
the love of your life yet,
it doesn't mean
they are not out there.

It just means
the time isn't right,
and timing in love,
is everything.

I won't judge you by the color
of your skin,
or by the clothes you wear,
but I will listen
for the truth in your words,
and the spirit of your laughter.

I will look for the light
in your eyes
that doesn't judge me,
and sees what is true
beyond words,
labels, and poems.

Listen
to what she says,
when she doesn't speak;

Know when to hold her,
and when to let her be.

Every day I am thankful for something
as simple as cold water,
a slice of pizza
or the way your voice calls me home.

And even when the world feels broken
and bent,
I am thankful for the people in my life,
and the life I've been given,

And even when I complain
the   way   humans   do,
because of our design,
I am still thankful.

I remember how small my
concerns are
against the infinite backdrop
of the universe,
and I watch
with a smile of gratitude,
as they disappear among the stars.

For a long time I confused love
with longing and desire,
and the need to always be thinking
about somebody, and for them
to always be thinking about me,
but lasting love is more of a slow
burning candle, than a forest fire.

It trusts deeply, and has no need
for drama or plot twists,
and it plays no games.

It's a genuine belief that this person
has been put in your path
because they embody everything
your soul needs to grow,
as you slowly heal each other's
childhood insecurities and
pain.

They are your best teacher,
and you're exactly
where you're supposed to be,
and will be, as long as you
continue to grow for yourself,
and for each other.

Words are only smoke,
when actions are the fire
that keeps us warm at night.

Whenever I hear your voice,
it's like a whisper of waves
crashing against an ocean
of silence,
and my ears become
like small sails unfurling
beneath the cloudy sky,
sailing in search of that sound.

It doesn't matter if
you say,

"Traffic jam."

"Radio."

Or, "cup of tea."

Whatever it is,
my love,
I will pick it up,
and carry it with me,
as if it were a song,
written only for me.

I want the day to go by slowly
with you and me,
laughing at how we used to be,
as the rain holds us in bed,
and the planet slowly turns like
a carousel in an abandoned
amusement park.

There is no way to reset the clock
or go back in time,
but through your laughter
and smile of grace,
defying all the seasons
in a single glance,
I can never grow old.

Hurt feelings,
if not grieved,
stay frozen
inside of us
long after the loss.

And if we're not careful,
we can become numb,
making the same mistakes
over and over,
until we're ready
to grieve the hurt,
and let the river flow
again,
so that the current
can take us
to where we belong.

I wasted so much time
wandering the streets in search
of something that would fill me
like the miracle of your kisses,
and the soft touch of your hand.

I wasted hours in daydreams,
writing poetry to the stars,
when all I wanted was for you
to find me, put your arms
around me,
and whisper something secret
in my ear.

Sometimes pain
leaves scars,
just so we remember
how we got them,
and never go back
that way again.

I cherish all the
moments
we spend together,
talking, laughing, kissing,
complaining,
losing ourselves in the oranges
of the afternoon sun.

Just look at the way the wind
loses itself
inside the trees,
making the branches
dance in the sunlight as
if by magic.

This is how you
make me feel
when I am with you.

The heart is given
more freely than the
soul,
because the heart
is temporary,
and the soul is forever.

That is why soulmates are
rare.

In order to truly move on,
you have to break
the old patterns that put
you there in the first
place.

So read, reflect,
talk to others,
so that you can learn
from your mistakes,
and learn to love
yourself the way you
deserve.

Then demand
nothing less
from others
in return.

And there are days it feels like
nothing ever changes,
days when you find yourself
standing on a ladder you
didn't even know you were
climbing

But from this vantage point
you can see how far you've come,
and how closer you are to living inside
the secret clouds of your dreams.

I want you to know
you bring a light to this world
that shines,
no matter how dark.

I want you to know
that there is somebody
who cherishes your smile,
and finds magic in your laughter.

I want you to know
that whatever happens,
you bring a light to this world,
and that is all that has ever mattered.

And in the end,
everybody is a poet
trying to figure out
how to love with words,
and capture the truth
of who we are,
so that somebody else
can read us,
understand us,
and love us
not just for what we
say,
but how we say it,

Don't tell me that you're lonely,
when the world is at your fingertips.

Open your eyes,
and see something old as new.

Look at the familiar,
until it becomes strange again.

Break away from your head
full of habits,
and smash the wine glass
until you can see the stars
that are always inside you.

See the miracle of this moment,
unfolding like a map of the universe
right in front of your eyes.

She was never
as lonely
as they believed.

She was the keeper
of a secret flame,
and she waited
patiently
for somebody
with eyes
to see it,
and love it,
as it burned.

Everybody has their own style
of healing, grieving, and
moving on.

And when you find yours,
don't let anybody tell you
it is anything less
than the most beautiful thing
on earth.

Put together your favorite books,
movies, poems, and songs,
and you will see how they reflect
the deepest parts of you.

The parts of you
that long for freedom from bullshit,
conformity, and fear.

The parts of you that are ready
to put away your guns,
and go home, because you
know nobody ever wins in war.

So find somebody
with love in their eyes,
and a place to call home.

Dig in the garden,
build something solid
for the kids to play on,
and pray for the blue sky
to go on forever.

"How will I know when
it's my soulmate?

"When time makes you
feel more and more sure,
they are the one."

In those early days
we had nothing but time,
young lovers, naked
and frail,
on beds as thin as paper.

Reading books,
drinking happy coffee,
laughing as the world
burned, and the sky
fell into the sea.

And just the touch
of your hand on
my skin,
was enough reason
to believe in miracles,
and even if these days
were numbered
like the pages in a novel,
they would always be beautiful
and worth reading again.

Open your heart to the rain
and the roses,
and the love that blooms
between the buildings
and beneath the concrete.

Be a flame of passion
burning with love,
and I promise
you will change the world,
just by being you.

I love to see your long hair
streaked with rain,
and to hear your footsteps
when you arrive at the door.

I love to take off your clothes,
as the rain falls,'
and the traffic slows,
and the sheets cool the skin.

I love to watch you as sleep comes on,
and you close our eyes,
disappearing into the city of our dreams,
where nobody can find us,
where we can be anyone,
where we can be us.

I kept reading these poetry books
hoping to find you folded
between the pages,
the way your body folds itself
into mine
on rainy nights
when we hide from the world
like children found in fairy tales,
leaving memories
like bread crumbs
in order to find
our
way
home.

Promise me you'll never
stop dreaming of love,
and that your eyes will
always fill with tears
at the sight of the ocean.

Never forget
the simple miracles
of life,
that pull us from the security
of the shore,
and into the infinite mystery
of the sea.

Remember I was the one
who walked with you
into the deep water,
and never looked back.

She's not perfect,
nor am I,
but isn't that
what makes us
human?

To me,
the most beautiful
thing about love,
is to know
no matter if she falls,
I will be there
to help her up,
and remind her
why I am here.

I fell for you
because I had no choice,
because when the sky opened
and the moon disappeared
into the starlit dream of your eyes,
I had no choice,
but to fall for you,
and keep falling
into
that mysterious paradise
where everyone
must fall
in order
to find
love.

She wants to feel all the love
breathing beneath your skin,
to taste the truth that opens
into the light of your smile,
and when nothing in this mad
and contradictory world
makes sense,
she wants you to connect
all the broken pieces,
and bring them back to her,
to show her they are still beautiful.

Soulmates
always
stay
because
they
have
found
what
they've
been
looking
for.

To be in love is to risk everything, because love is everything.

Love with her
is a perpetual mystery,
a game of invention and reinvention,
making memories from the simple
ingredients of life,
small-town carnivals,
and seaside shops,
places where she can put a feather
in her hair, and pretend to be a pirate,
as she turns everything ordinary
into a vast and mysterious ocean,
with just the curve of her smile.

So much love gets lost
in the clutter and noise of everyday,
and in the echo of everything
demanding our attention,
and expecting us to be a certain way.

You must listen for love
in the quiet places
where nobody else is listening,
and look for love
in the ordinary places
where nobody else is looking,
and I promise you will be amazed
at the love you find.

If you still don't believe
in true love,
look at that old couple
holding hands
in the park,
and ask yourself,
what is the light
you see
in their eyes?

Even after I'd got it all together,
and quit the drinking and the dying,
I felt an emptiness like a cold stone
inside of me, a desire for something
without a name; and I went on about
my days, reading books and drinking
coffee and day dreaming of other lives
I might live.

And then one day you arrived,
without warning, like a wind storm
or a winning lottery ticket or fate
wearing lipstick and blue jeans,
and suddenly your name filled me
like a million love poems,
and I knew there was some magic in
this universe you can't control.

You can only wait and walk and dream,
until it finds you, and it will find you
when you are ready, and not a moment
earlier, and when it does, you will be
surprised and not surprised,
because some things
feel already written in the stars,
before we even know their name.

To be continued…

About the Author:

Mark Anthony is a bestselling poet from Seattle, Washington whose previous works include, "The Beautiful Truth," "The Beautiful Life," "Love Notes," and "True Love."

He is happily married to his soulmate and continues to live the life of his dreams by following the map of his heart.

You can follow him on Instagram:
@markanthonypoet

And Facebook:
@markanthonypoet

Printed in Great Britain
by Amazon